JANET GORDON

I SEE YOU GIRL

A COLLECTION OF POEMS CELEBRATING LIFE'S GREATEST COMEBACKS

I SEE YOU, GIRL

JANET GORDON

ISBN: 978-1-7770093-0-4

Printed in Canada

© Copyright by Janet Gordon

Sister, My Sister

Sister, my sister, so put together

Everything from the outside says, "I am alright"

But inside it's a fight

Others see me and tell me how good I look, and how they wish they could look as good as me

But I just shake it off

After all, I don't even like me

Sister, my sister, can't you see that my dressing

like this is a cry for help, not for style

I go home, and I cry

Some days, I just want to scream

Sister, my sister, please read between the lines

When you talk to me, I don't even look you in the eyes

My eyes are always to the ground, just like how I feel

Sister, my sister, let us keep it real; you, too, now how I feel.

Happy International Women's Day

We celebrate our achievements and accomplishments. We celebrate our failures and our comebacks. We are a movement that is strong and resilient. We have strength in numbers, as we move forward. We resist all negatives and celebrate the positives. We may have far to go to catch up with our male counterparts, but we are doing it together, reaching higher heights, standing on each other's shoulders, gleaning from each other's strength. We are bridge-builders, advocating for equal rights, equal pay, and equal opportunities, while bearing our burdens. Many are blind to our plights. Some want to portray us as catty, undermining, and useless, but we stand together today lifting our banner that says, "Sisterhood, strength, dignity, grace, excellence, peace, health, love, joy, fierce, beauty, and purpose." We are our own individuals, unique in our strength, gathering today and standing powerfully in unity. We are a force to reckon with. We stand for those who are beaten down and have lost their voices. We stand for those that illness has defeated. We stand for those whose children have been taken away. We stand for those that have lost hope, we stand for those that have been marginalized, stigmatized, and stereotyped.

We stand for those that have stopped dreaming, and we encourage you to dream again yes you dream again we stand for those that are struggling with infertility, battling with mental illness, oppression and depression. We celebrate your openness to change, we celebrate diversity, and we push each other to great success, whether in technology, science, media, inventions, or creativity. We are trainers and builders of our communities. Whatever our platform or area of influence, we stand as sisters, mothers, grandmothers, great-grandmothers, aunts, grandaunts, cousins, and friends. We are women.

Crying Woman

Hold your belly and cry

Weeping is not forever; your joy will come

Crying woman, don't waste your time wondering "Why me?"

Crying woman, keep your faith and your strength

Your tears will not be in vain

Crying woman, we surround you with our love

Every beginning must have an end

Crying woman, do not lose your strength

I wrote this poem while watching television and seeing a woman crying over the loss of a loved one.

I See You

I see you splatter

But your heart is still beating

I see you broken but not defeated

I see you

I see your eyes still sparkle when someone says, "I love you"

I see you heal and become new again

I see you walking and talking

I see you beautiful and strong

I see you fulfilling your dreams and helping to make others' dreams come true

I see you making a difference in this big world

I see you being so blessed

I see you becoming the best mother that you can be

My sister, I see you

This poem is about not losing hope, even when it is dark.

I Love Your Flaws and All

I love your flaws and all

I love your quirkiness You are the best

You are critical of yourself

Self-hate is cruelty to oneself when you can't get away from yourself.

I love your flaws and all

You are unique and cute

Yeah, you are cute

I love your flaws and all

I love to see you trying to stand straight for me, because you have been teased about your knocked-knees all your life

I love you just the way you are

You were created and fashioned for me

I am in love with you, all of you

You are always in the mirror and on your phone, checking out yourself, finding faults with yourself

Don't you know that you are a masterpiece? I wouldn't change anything about you

I love your flaws and all.

Complaining about the space between your front teeth

My queen, that was one of the things that attracted me to you Your smile plays the melody of my heart and causes my heart to beat

I love your flaws and all.

I Am Strong

Accepting the challenge to be strong, I am taking my life and future in my hands. I know what I want, and I know what works best for me. I am strong, not because I can lift heavy weights; I am strong because I choose to live, and I believe in myself and all that is inside of me. I am utilizing all the gifts and talents that I was blessed with. You may not see my gifts as having any value, but they do. I know that I am living the life that I was designed to live

each day. I am living my best life daily. I am transformed by renewing the truth and reality of who I am—

I am a woman, daughter, cousin, aunt, friend, and wife. Each of those titles help to form the person that I am evolving into.

I choose to have joy daily and to celebrate my victories, whether they are big or small. I am strong.

Unstoppable You

Unstoppable you,

Yes, you, I am talking to you.

You are unstoppable.

Your life is about to turn around for the better.

You have been going through a massive storm, and you feel like everything has turned upside-down in your life.

You are unstoppable, girl.

Don't allow your current situation to determine how your future will look.

You are alive, you are not under the ground.

You are unstoppable, yes, you,

Your life can, and will, turn around.

Do you hear me? You are unstoppable.

"If I am unstoppable, then how come I am living in a shelter?" she asks. "How come I am sleeping on my friend's couch?"

Don't you know that many of the greatest and biggest stars started where you are? Read the memoirs of people of influence, and you will truly believe that you are unstoppable.

It's not how you started, it's how you will finish, and you will finish strong and victorious, because you are unstoppable.

Keep your dream alive. Don't give up on yourself. Dreams do come true. You will move from the prison to the palace, and sooner than you think. Keep confessing truth over your life; it will change your life for the better.

First Date

You asked me what my first impression of you was.

I told you that I thought you were self-obsessed, a great dresser, and a person that seemed to love herself very much.

You became upset with me.

You told me that one of your pet peeves was people who are phony, and that you love and respect honesty.

You said that you work hard for what you've got,

But that was my first impression of you.

First date, will there be another?

We sat in silence while you played on your phone.

The waiter asked if we wanted dessert, but you say no, you want to go home. That wasn't how I envisioned this evening ending.

First date, wow, first impression,

"I like you, and I want to get to know you," I said.

You finally looked up from your phone and asked, "You want to get to know me? I, who you think is self-obsessed?"

I chimed in with, "And a great dresser and a person who loves herself, and if you love yourself, then you will be able to love me someday.

I am looking for a woman that knows her worth, confident, not conceited, loving, generous, beautiful, honest, respectful, humble, and kind.

I want to get to know you."

First date, will there be another?

You call our server over to our table and say that it seems we will be staying, after all. I found out that we were both cheesecake lovers.

Time was suspended as we got to know each other. Beautiful first date of many.

She Stand

Every Day She Stands

She stands and faces life's challenges.

She rises to every occasion, and never blinks.

She believes in herself, even when she stands alone.

She uses strategies and insights in her daily life. She makes her plans, and her life is centered on the Great I Am.

She knows what challenges to accept and which ones to let go of.

Many call her lucky, but she knows that is not what it is.

She knows that whatever the circumstances are, she always gives it to the Great I Am, because that is where she stands.

Rocking

Big girls rock. We must do a recap. We can't allow them to stop us, because we are big girls and we rock. We are human beings, and we have rights. One size doesn't fit all, so stop trying to fit us in your box. I am a big girl, and I rock. You call us fat, but this is our normal. We are not outsiders; we are human. Many of us are healthy, wealthy, and strong. We are confident being this size. We are big girls, and we rock, calling for a replay, oh yeah.

Beautiful, Flawed, Broken Soul

Beautiful, flawed soul can't accept love. Rejected and broken from the womb when mama spoke over you that she didn't want you or your daddy. You were that constant reminder of pain, so she took you to Grandma, and never returned. Beautiful, flawed, broken soul can't love anyone, not even herself. Saying daily to her younger self, "I am not worthy of being loved. I look just like Mama, and she doesn't love me. Not realizing that Mama too is broken and flawed and can't love at all. Wipe your tears, child, because Mama is wounded and afraid. She has never trusted the word love. When she was a teenager, she was molested by a person who said that he loved her and would never hurt her. He was supposed to protect her, not molest her. Her ideas of love are tainted. To her, love had taken away her most precious gift—her virginity. It was forcefully taken away from her, and when she told her loved ones what had happened to her, they called her a troublemaker. After all, Uncle would never do that to his niece. Beautiful, flawed, broken soul, trying to bring shame upon the family name, just like her mother. What they didn't realize was that history was repeating itself, because they hadn't dealt with the past. It was swept under the rug, and now there is a bulge that can't be hidden. Mama has been mourning her loss ever since. Even though you look like Mama, and everyone can see it, she doesn't see it. What she sees when she sees you is the day that her life changed.

Beautiful, flawed, broken soul. Now you have a baby girl, too. What are you going to do? You have walked out on the man that you vowed to love, until death do you part, with baby in hand. Beautiful, flawed, broken soul, what are you going to do? Now your husband is suing you for custody of his daughter, calling you an unfit mother, and saying you are just like your mama. Your family is saying, "Don't allow what happened to your mother to happen to your daughter." Beautiful, flawed, broken soul, what are you going to do?

Never Ever Will I Dim My Light

Never ever will I dim my light so you can shine because of your insecurities.

I am a light called to be a light by the Great I Am.

I am chosen. I will not decrease so your ego can increase.

I am beautiful and wonderful, whether you agree or not.

I am loving, tenacious, and strong. I am helpful and hopeful.

I am creative and courageous. I am a builder of positive bridges.

I tear down negative walls.

I am progressive and outgoing.

Never ever will I dim my light, so you can shine because of your insecurity.

I am excited about life every day.

I am a giver of love. I lead tribes of women to greatness and their full potential.

I am a voice for the voiceless.

I am strength for those that are weak.

Yeah, I refuse to dim my light and my life for you to shine for all the wrong reasons.

I am a change generator.

I am living my life of purpose and grace.

I am an influencer, and I inspire others to achieve their full potential.

Never ever will I dim my light so you can shine.

I am salt. I am needed to make things better.

I am a change maker. Never ever will I dim my light for you to shine.

Knocked Down But Not Out

Don't count me out yet,

I am just down temporarily.

If I have breath, I am still fighting.

I am a warrior.

I am victorious.

I am fierce.

I am not frightened.

They are counting down, but I am not out.

I will live to fight again.

Seasons change; I am in my winning season.

Knocked down but won't stay down.

Don't celebrate your victory yet,

This is just a temporary setback.

Every setback leads to a greater comeback.

Victory is mine.

I retrieve it.

You can't have my identity.

I am victorious.

I can't be defeated.

Knocked down but not knocked out.

I may be bruised and broken, but never defeated.

I won't retreat. I am a fighter for life.

I am a winner. I refuse to stay down.

I am victorious.

I am not who you say that I am.

I am victorious. You can't control or rule me.

Still Standing

Still standing, despite all the blockages, chaos, ridicule, dragging my name all over the internet.

I am still standing.

I am standing, because you will never have the power to defeat and destroy me.

I am standing, because you have thrown me your best shot and missed terribly.

I am still standing, because your hatred for me could not overpower me.

I am standing, because I am a queen, born to reign and you can't change that.

I am standing, because I have unmasked you, and you can no longer hide from me.

I am standing.

Forever My Sister

They say that sisters come in all variations and colours.

There are many ways to spell the word sister, but one thing remains the same:

It is the true meaning of sister that describes you. You are an original, authentic. You are my sister forever. You are extremely confident and quick to forgive.

You are loving, kind, generous, honest, beautiful, gifted, victorious, and fierce.

I value you as my sister and friend. You celebrate my victory with me, and encourage me when I am down. I am grateful to have you. You are a beautiful flower that keeps blooming.

I love you, and I love the way you care about your family and friends. You always have my back.

Yes, you are that sister that brings light.

You're always there to encourage, motivate, and lead by example. You don't have to prove anything to anyone.

You are very important and special to me. I love spending time with you. You are strong and courageous.

I love to hear and see your laughter; you bring happiness in this world.

I can't imagine my life without you in it. You are fierce and unstoppable.

I love texting you and talking to you; you get my weird sense of humour. Your posting on social media is positive and influential,

though sometimes we have our differences.

You are always there for me, standing and cheering me on.

Having you as my sister brings joy to my heart. You will always be a part of me. You're a beautiful soul. I love shopping, reading, and hanging out with you, trending and styling all the time. I love your honesty and loyalty.

I love and respect you. You are my forever sister.

Lady At The Lake

She sits watching and searching the faces of those passing by.

Each face tells its own unique story.

She sits alone, mesmerized by the flow of the water.

The smile on her face merges with the afternoon sun.

The sounds of the water soothe her soul, as she walks back and forth according to the movement of the water.

Beauty, health, strength, and confidence radiate from her like the sun shines.

She is in love with nature and its beauty.

She appreciates the things in life that others overlook.

She takes out her iPad and takes some pictures, then listens to music that she has downloaded.

She fills the pages of her journal with her thought for the day.

Her dreams and desires have been fulfilled for today.

She is an excellent listener, and her ears and eyes pay attention when you are speaking.

She gives her heart to the people.

Everyone wants to talk to her and become her friend.

People are drawn to her as steel to magnet or bees to a hive.

Men want to get to know her, and women want to be just like her.

I wrote this poem at the lake with my hubby.

I Am Rooting For You

I am rooting for you. I see that you are trying to make a difference in your family and your community. I am cheering you along. I believe in you. Don't give up. I am standing with you. You have started over so many times; I admire that you have never given up. I am your biggest fan. I am celebrating you. You don't allow what others are saying about you to affect your trying. You are giving hope to those that only know how to give up. I am rooting for you. I believe in you. You are resilient and strong. You have many plans. You don't depend on anyone. You are a woman that loves to spread her wings and be a boss lady. Even those that are talking behind your back want to be like you. You know your role, and you relish in it; you are amazing at it. I am rooting for you. You siege opportunities when they present themselves. You are valuable to your community and your sisters. Individuals hear about you before they meet you. You're a legend in our community.

Yeah, I am rooting for you. You have overcome many obstacles, and you keep trying. It is a pleasure to know you. Many have asked me why I admire you so much. I reply, "She never gives up. She is a go-getter." I am cheering you on. I appreciate you and all that you do. You have your own branding, and no one can duplicate your styles.

You're a legend in your field. You provide exceptional service to your clients. They are committed, and they respect you. You are always thinking and making a new move. You surround yourself with those that are well connected and strong. Your life is in the public's eyes, and many have their misconceptions about you, but I am rooting for you.

I See You

I see that you have been crushed and splattered, left for dead.

But your heart is still beating.

I see you broken but not defeated.

I see you.

I see your eyes still sparkle when someone says, "I love you."

I see you heal and become new again.

I see you walking and talking.

I see your beauty and your strength.

I see you fulfilling your dreams and helping to make others' dreams come true

I see you making a difference in this big world.

I see you being so blessed.

I see you becoming the best mother that you can be.

My sister, I see you and I love you.

My Daughter, I Love You

Daughter of mine, I love you so much.

My heart yearns for you each day.

I am a blessed mother to have you as my daughter.

I love you.

Your love is like an embrace and a good force around me.

Your presence fills my heart with joy.

You have given of yourself to others, unconditionally.

I am proud to call you my daughter and my friend.

My daughter and friend, until we meet again.

Warrior Sister

You are a warrior standing for truth,

Wearing your warrior gear,

Your presence burns like fire when the enemy sees you.

Warrior sister, you are fierce and strong,

Gentle when needed.

Concluding that I am no longer a victim,

I am a victorious warrior,

Rising above every setback that has been sent my way,

Not seeking anyone's approval, trusting in the truth I know.

You won't put me down anymore, just to elevate yourself.

I have confidence in me. I am proud of who I've become through this tragedy,

Knowing that my sisters are standing as a mighty army of women surrounding and believing in me.

Believe in you.

Girl, Bye

Girl, bye.

You are background noise. I have moved on, so should you. You tell everyone that will listen that you're over me. If you're over me, then why are you still talking about me?

Girl, bye.

Stop trying to waste my time. You're the one that said I was not what you were looking for.

Girl, bye. If I wasn't good enough for you, then why all the noise? I discovered that my moving on with my life has caused you to be bitter, but made me better. Girl, bye. What I have found is exactly what I was looking for—an authentic, transparent, dynamic woman who was tired of the games and was looking for real love. Girl, bye. You are clearly afraid of commitment; you chose to run away.

Girl, bye.

No more drama. I made time for myself, and realize that I need to dream bigger and change my habits. Girl, bye. You are leaving me. I was the best gift you gave me. Girl, bye.

Don't be someone's side chick,

when you can be the star of your own show. I'm sick and tired of playing the game, fooling myself that you were the one for me. Boy, please, I am not sending you any more money. You're a grown man. I deserve to be loved by someone that loves me, and I am the star of his feature film. I have been generous to you, and you have been selfish.

Boy, please, I am ready to start something else.

The Girl that Didn't Love Her Real Hair

She used her hoodie to cover her hair in class, because everyone asked, "What's up with your hair? Didn't you just get your hair done? Let us see your new hairstyle." For three days, no one could see her hair, not even her bestie. Curiosity got the best of me. I intervened and asked, "What is really going on with your hair?" She hesitated. Then, as if she was worn out with all the questions over the past three days, she said, "I miss my weave." I thought I hadn't heard what she had said. She whispered, "My mother did my hair, but without weave, so I don't want anyone to see my real hair, because I don't like it."

Age seven.

Strong

Accepting the challenge to be strong, I am taking my life and future in my hands. I know what I want, and I know what works best for me. I am strong, not because I can lift heavy weights; I am strong because I choose to live, and I believe in myself and all that is inside of me. I am utilizing all my gifts and talents that I was blessed with. You may not see my gifts as gifts, but they are. I know that they are.

Sounds

I am a trumpet, I make sounds.

My sounds are loud and sometimes soft,

I am special and round.

I am a trumpet, I love my sound.

My sounds are unique, and they shake the ground.

I am a trumpet, I love my own sound.

My sound can be gentle and soothing, but it's my sound.

Feeling Free

I understand that you never knew what it meant to celebrate someone else. I am making old new again, commanding insecurity to let go of me.

I'm done fighting with people's opinions of me. I'm not fighting with you. I am confident, and I am filled with love. I trust others and myself. I am using my voice to advocate for change in this world. I am free, and with freedom comes responsibility. My journey was blocked by my own thoughts that led to my actions. I am living my new life with passion and purpose.

I have something that is special and powerful. My gifts are undeniable. My insecurities are no more.

My Story

You don't know my story.

You are living with me, but you don't know me.

I am not defined by my condition or my situation.

My story has many endings. You don't know my story.

Why am I smoking? It soothes my pain.

But the root of my pain is deep.

You don't know my story.

Each day feels like a never-ending storm, but I know that I must go on.

Telling my story may just help someone.

Now you know part of my story.

Trouble

"Who is that?" she asks.

That's just Trouble.

Is her name Trouble?

Yes, her name is Trouble.

How can someone name their child Trouble?

I must ask her a question: Who is Trouble?

How does it feel to have a name like Trouble, and to have everyone call you Trouble?

Well, when your name is Trouble, no one troubles you.

Dream Blocker, Dream Stopper

Advice to myself: Don't need anyone more than they need you.

Don't be a doormat, be a door, a door of greatness, opportunities, and blessing.

Advice to myself: Life has four seasons. If you are in a season of drought, you are one decision away from a new season.

Winter never lasts forever. Spring is on its way, and it can't be stopped.

Chaos and turmoil won't last forever. Peace is your inheritance, so go after it.

Remember that you will become what you think about.

Advice to myself: Love yourself, take care of yourself, make peace with yourself.

Love others always, and walk in love, even when an individual doesn't deserve it.

Remove all self-imposed limitations. Give your mind permission to soar like an eagle.

Set goals and follow through. Be a student always, and never say, "I am too old to learn."

Never stop trying. You don't always have to do it right; just get it done.

Advice to myself: Speak the truth, even when it is not popular. Stand up for someone who can't stand up for themselves.

Don't be afraid of some people's opinions, and remember that you have an option.

Dream big, and remember, many will laugh at your dream and think that it is too big or just plain stupid, but don't give up.

Little Miss Innocent

She has three sides.

She will say what you want to hear,

Be who you want her to be, only when she is around you.

She knows, and practices, how to get you in her hook or her web.

Everyone knows her as a different person.

She is a little miss innocent to her family. She is an undercover bad girl.

Boyfriends don't know that there are many of them.

She knows how to play the game, because she runs the game.

What?

What are you looking at?

Is it my hair, or my shoe?

What are you looking at?

Is it the way I try to appear confident?

Or is it my word in action?

What are you looking at?

Is it the way I try to make everyone like me?

Or is it the way I talk above everyone to get all the attention for myself?

What are you looking at?

Is it the way I put down everyone and exalt myself?

Yeah, what are you looking at?

Don't Follow Me

You are following me, basing your lifestyle on me.

I don't know who I am anymore. I am a product, a manufacturer's commodity.

I don't understand my new self. Don't copy me; I was a program to make money.

Money is all I see and know.

Money is never too much for me.

When I lend my name to endorse products, I don't have to use or like the product; it's all about the money.

Don't look up to me or tell me that I am spoiling your child. Your child is your responsibility.

I am acting; it's not reality, so don't throw the blame on me.

Whatever I do, I do it for money, honey.

Can't Satisfy You

I will never be enough for you. Trying to satisfy you is only momentary.

If I give you my last breath, it still would not be good enough for you. I can never please you.

Pleasing you is only momentary. Whatever you want from me, I am not able to give it to you. I love you, and I will continue to show, and give, you love. I will continue to give you my best. I hope that you will eventually see that I am doing, and giving you, my best. I finally have peace about this situation. I realize that there is a fight within you, and the struggle is within you, and when you are lashing out at me, you are looking for ease from the pain within. You have the power inside of you to win this inner battle. Because I won't ever be enough for you.

Oh No,

OH NO, HE DIDN'T SAY THAT

Oh no, you need to go. Did you just call me a whore?

Last night I was on fleek, your queen, now I am a whore?

Asking me to forgive you again.

Last time you called me stupid, and told me I knew nothing, and I did forgive you again.

I put it behind me, as if it never happened. Now I am a whore. I am asking you a question: How much did it cost you to be with me? I am asking you a question. Since you won't answer, I will. It didn't cost you anything, but it cost me my pride, self-respect, insecurities, depression, and low self-esteem. You don't love me. Love covers. Love protects. The words you are telling me don't represent love to me. It doesn't matter what you are telling me, because you want me to stay. I won't; I am going my own way.

Lying Is What You Do.

Lying is what you do. I don't need you. We are through.

I see that when your cell phone rings, you take it to the washroom.

And you suddenly turn the pipe on to drown out your conversation. I believe that you are convinced that I am a fool. Guess what?

I see you.

I see that my texts and phone calls are ignored. And when I ask you about it, it's all excuses of why you couldn't respond. I see you.

I see that you are working later and later, telling me that you are working on special projects, but your pay remains the same. Hey, guess what? I see   you.
Every weekend, you are spending more time with your boys and less time with me. Honey, I see   you.
I see that you have given our love and our dreams to someone new. I am tired of asking you, "What's going on?" I am asking you questions that I already know the answers to. I don't need you. We are through. Lying is what you do. I see you.

You Can't Love Me

You are both looking for love.

You keep complaining about how he doesn't understand you,

That he doesn't appreciate you and all that you do for him.

My sister, he can't give you what he doesn't have.

He, too, is looking for someone to love him.

He doesn't know how to be a husband; he only knows how to be a son.

Daddy wasn't a word he used to know. He has no training how to be the husband that you want him to be.

He needs love, too. He doesn't even realize that something is missing in his life.

He is disconnected. He can't give you what you have been missing.

Love Heals

Take your eye off your past, and look toward your future.

The street of regret can be a long, winding road, full of fake exits and fake entrances.

Don't be easily irritated, for if the wounds of the past are irritated, it means you are not fully healed.

Why do we feel so entitled to our wound? We feel like it is a badge of honor.

Instead, believe that things will change, and accept help when the help is offered and genuine. But too much help can cripple you. Love heals a broken person, if they allow the love to flow, and apply love as a medicine that heals the soul.

Your Love Answers Me

When love answers the call, wake up with renewed strength, feeling new anticipation, like something exciting is about to happen today. Love comes chasing after me on my way to the mall. We bump into each other in the parking lot. We both say, "Sorry, I wasn't looking where I was going." We stand there, looking at each other. I feel things in my body that I didn't know were still working. My feet cannot move. Our eyes stay locked, while your hand still holds mine. Neither of us wants to move. Finally, you ask me, "Where were you rushing off to?" I try to gather my composition, and I stutter, "I was going to the library in the mall." You introduce yourself as Paul, and ask if I would like to have coffee with you. I say, "Yes, I would love to. My name is Sophie. Thanks for bumping into me. I don't drink coffee; I love tea." Love comes chasing   after   me.

Will You be Mine?

I asked you to be my wife, because I can't see myself living without you in my life. I knew that you were the one for me when we stayed on the phone all night, talking and texting. You got me. I went to bed with you on my mind and woke up with you on my mind.

I asked you to be my wife, because I knew, and appreciated, the gift and treasure that I found. I am not rushing things! I just found what I was searching for. Will you be mine?

On my knee, with an engagement ring in my hand, you looked with amazement toward my hand. At first, I thought that you didn't hear me, so I repeated, "Will you marry me?"

Your answer was, "Why me? You can have any woman. Why me?" I replied, "I found what I was searching for. I don't need to keep looking." My answer seemed to please you. You said, "Yes, I will marry you." She said yes.

Love Says Hello

His name was Roy, short and stubby,

Handsome, dark, sweet chocolate for me, that is what I thought.

I would always volunteer to go to the grocery store, just to walk past his house and catch a glimpse of him.

My friends would laugh at me, because whenever I saw him, and he said, "Hello,"

I would be love-struck and lose my voice. Whenever he went away, I would know exactly what I would say, if only he were here.

When they would tease me and call me his girlfriend, he would deny me.

Now that I am all grown up and blooming in all the right places, he is sending me his digits.

Sorry, I am not trying to make him pay for all men's downfalls and mistakes, but I did love him very much, and he could not reciprocate my love. He is not responsible for my decision. I have grown out of love with him.

Addiction

I am addicted to you,

Can't get enough of you,

Can't put you away, I am always holding you in my hand.

Your love for me is real and true.

You love me for who I am, and you never criticize me.

You allow me to be me, and I am obsessed with you. I love you.

When and where I need you, you are always there for me.

It doesn't matter what mode I am in, you support me. You never say a word to make me upset. You are the best. My friends are jealous of our relationship. They are all saying that we are too close.

They don't understand how you make me feel; you fill all my voids.

You know and keep all my secrets; I can even trust you with all my passwords.

I love you, my cell phone.

Mama

Mama, I love you. I love your grace, your wisdom, and your love. To call you my mother is one of God's blessings in my life. You are always there for me, even when I wasn't making wise choices. You have supported my dreams and have shown me, by example, how to follow my dreams. You are my queen.

You respect my decisions and allow me to find and follow my path. I love you, my mama. Thank you for always having my back and being a tower of strength for me.

You're a great role model for me and many others. As I am faced with daily life decisions, I often wonder what would Mama do? Then I call or text you, and the answer would flow through. You are in the know. When you are faced with adversity, you face life head-on. You are not afraid to speak and stand for your truth, even when it means that you will not be liked. First, you were having challenges with technology. You would always ask how to use your laptop or computer. I convinced you to face your fear of technology and take some computer courses, and now you are a master of email and texting. I love how you are always trending and have a massive following on Facebook. You are a fashionista, and everyone always wants to see what you are wearing. You're relevant and fierce, Mama. I love you. I will tell you how much I love you while you are still living. I love hearing your voice and laughter, they make me happy.

Trying To Figure Out Love

I am trying to figure out this thing called love. You are the new girl in the neighborhood, and every guy wants to get to know you. You reach out to me. We have been hanging out, but I still don't know what this love thing is all about. I've never seen love in action before, only on TV, and it comes with misery, drama, and heartaches. I want you to always show me affection, on public display, for others to see that you are with me.

You say that you love me, and I think I love you, too. How do I know if our love is for real? I am still figuring out this thing called love. Now you're telling me that we are going to have a baby that will need our love, so I better figure out what love is fast, because our baby will need love from both of us. Baby is here and needs our care and love, no time for ourselves. Still trying to figure out this thing called love.

I Found You

You are what I have been searching for.

The void in my heart has been refilled. My heart has been yearning for you and seeking you.

My heart used to miss a beat, but now that I have found you, my heart is beating in perfect rhythm. As I am looking ahead, all I am seeing is brighter days. You are what I have been searching for. Now that my heart is beating right, my dreams are being fulfilled every day. It is a new beginning.

Yes, you are what I was searching for. Waking up each day used to be a waste of time, now I can't wait to spend time with you, I am loving our lazy days as we look for unique places to have breakfast. I love when we pack our picnic basket and spend our day at the lake, watching the water in silence. Yes, you are all I have been searching for.

Happiness

My happiness doesn't depend on you.

My happiness comes from within me.

Having money doesn't make someone happy; it is just a deposit to our happiness.

How we use that money will determine our happiness. Are we using our money to bless others? Or is it all about us?

Material things won't make us happy; they may for a little while, but then we will go back to being unfulfilled, again.

Love your Creator, love yourself. As we do both, we will be able to love others in return.

When we walk in love, we will live longer, and we will be the light that attracts others.

Let us strengthen our love walk; it is one of the best decisions we will ever make.

My Son

Too soon you were taken from me, but God must have a better plan for you.

Heaven must need an angel with a beautiful smile like yours.

Though your life was brief, your memory will live forever.

Your love for your family, everyone can see.

You were a friend to your friends, a good brother to your sister, I know that you will keep a watch over her always.

When I see your son, his face is like looking in your face.

It's a pity you had to die.

My pledge to you is that I will take good care of your son.

Things that I never had time to do with you, I will make sure to do with your son.

This time around, I will play when he wants to play,

I will read to him when he wants someone to read to him.

Your son will know that he is well-loved.

You are my love child.

As God is first in my life, my family second to God, I will live a balanced life. My son, your death will not be in vain.

I will teach other mothers and fathers about what I have learned and the mistakes that I have made.

My plans for you were to see you finish high school and go on to college or university,

Be a good father to your son, and walk down the aisle at your wedding.

I never doubted that as I grew old, you would take care of me.

I know the son I trained and taught you to be.

I know that someday you would have made a good husband. And even though you did it in reverse, that, too, was a part of God's master plans.

Today, Lord, bring good from this tragedy.

In this troubled time, let your love and peace sustain me.

Wedding Day

How do I let you go, my daughter?

As I help you dress on your wedding day, I can't help but think that it seems like just yesterday I took you home from the hospital. Then it was the first day of school.

We had many celebrations and events along the way, many school dances, and, of course, your prom. I know that I must let you grow up and live your life. As I waved you off to college, then university, I knew that you were ready to start your new life. On one of your visits, you came home with a new friend. We knew that it was more than a friendship; we saw how you both looked at each other. After your graduation, he asked your dad and me for your hand in marriage.

Today is your wedding day. As I watch your bridesmaids fuss over you, you turn around and ask, "Mom, do you have something blue?" only to see me with happy tears in my eyes. You gently wipe my tears away. I take your veil and place it on your head. "You're a beautiful bride," I said. "I am so glad that God has blessed us with you."

You ask me if there were any last words of wisdom I had to give to you. I said, "Let God and prayer be first in your life, always give love, never go to bed angry, talk to your husband about whatever you're not happy with, and remember you are now one."

The piano started to play "Here Comes the Bride." You kissed me and held me so tight, it was a hug that I will always remember. You whisper in my ear, "I am ready to start my new life."

I stood on the side as your father came to take hold of your hand. He had been dreaming about walking you down the aisle.

The minister asked, "Who gives this woman away?" I said to myself, "I am loaning her to him. I could never truly give her away."

We both said, "We do," and with broken hearts, we hand you over to your husband-to-be.

As you repeated your vows that you wrote to each other, so full of love, I wept for myself, my loss, and my gain.

At the reception, in my speech, I told stories of a happy time, and passed on my advice, "Let love and prayer be your foundation. Never go to bed angry."

Lazy Love

As I got out of bed this morning, I stood to look out my window.

The trees were still sleeping, the water was dancing,

The birds were singing beautiful songs of love and never-ending happiness.

As I walked to the balcony overlooking the water,

I said, "Good morning, Father. Thank you for giving me life today."

I hear the ocean calling me, letting me know it is alive.

The seagulls, feeling left out, started to sing their best morning songs.

I slip on my slippers to walk down to the seashore. The beat of the waves splashes at my feet. I stand in awe of God's handiworks.

Wish You Were Here

Surrounded by beautiful turquoise water reminds me of you.

I take our usual walk along the boardwalk, feeling out of place without you.

Everyone has a partner, holding hands, or just friends taking a stroll.

I sit at our favorite rock, with my feet in the water, listening to waves. How I wish you were here.

The sun starts to go down and makes its exit for the day. I wish you were here.

Lazy summer music comes from the café, as couples gather around dancing the time away. Oh, how I wish you were here.

The party boat goes around the harbors, with merry people having a good time. I wish you were here.

Raindrops, Rainfalls

Dedicated to my husband, Danny. You inspire me.

The rain splashes against the windowpane,

I press my face to the glass looking for you,

Wondering when you will come home, my love.

The sound of the rain on the rooftop beats like drums beating to the rhythm of my heart. Where are you, my love? I need to feel your nearness as my second skin.

Our favorite song plays on the stereo. I put it on repeat. The words say, "This place is empty without you, my baby."

I hear the door opening. I look around to see you standing there, soaking wet, from head to toe.

I pull you inside. "Let me get you warm, my love." As I help you to take your wet clothes off,

Your body glistens against the light from the fireplace.

Raindrops, rainfalls, always get me in the mood for love.

You Say That You Are In Love With Me

You said that you love me, so why is it that my private pictures, which were for your eyes only, are all over the internet? How is this love? You are destroying me and pulling me down. This is the last straw; I am done. I have had my eyes black and blue, my lips busted, those eyes that you called dreamy and my lips you called juicy were busted by your hands, the same hands that caressed me.

You say that you love me and that you would give your life for me. How is it that the paramedic had to resuscitate me, because you knocked the life out of me? Your actions and your words are not the same. You said that you love me and that I am the best thing that ever happened to you, so why do you keep hurting and abusing me?

Love

Love can have many sides and many shades, many heights, and many depths. For many individuals, love can mean protection, love can mean provision, love can mean security. Even though we love to hear someone say, "I love you," some would rather be shown love. Love is an action word. "I love you," can heal old wounds, and it can also cause new wounds. Telling someone that you love them can save and change a person's life. Love can brighten your day. Having someone to love you endlessly every day, even when you are not always at your best, can bring out the best in you. Love can be sweet, and it can make you bitter. Love can bring, and give, you joy. When the word love is used in action, it will create an explosion of newness, because love is creative. Love is positive. Love heals. When you are loved deeply and passionately, you will blossom and become that rare flower that blooms, and it will attract those that never used to see you before. Love brings out the best in us. Love chases away darkness. Love will take you on the journey of love.

I Found Myself

The day I found myself, I didn't know that I was lost, until I found myself.

I didn't realize that parts of me were missing, until pieces of me were found.

Tiny, broken, missing pieces have been restored, bit by bit. I may still look broken, but I have been restored from the inside out.

I have been enlightened by a new passion that is flowing in my life. Renewed fire is blazing within me, taking me to peaks and heights I have never experienced before.

I found myself, even though I didn't realize that I was missing.

My Queen

I know that at times you feel invisible, and all your life you have been told that you are not good enough.

You are known as the black sheep of the family, and you have believed that lie.

You were traumatized by those who were supposed to protect and love you. You were never told that you were good for something.

I have listened to your stories of loss and abuse, when I was growing up.

Today I want you to know that you are my queen, and I love, respect, honor, and adore you. You're the best mother for me, and you have done your very best.

You guide me in many ways. The sacrifices that you have made for me and my siblings are not in vain.

I love you. You have shown us what unconditional love looks like.

You were taught not to love your skin tone. I love your beautiful, dark chocolate skin; you can wear any colour clothing.

You have impeccable style, and you're an amazing mother and friend. When I was growing up, all my friends wished that you were their mother.

I admire your resilience and your love for life.

I want you to know that your hair is good hair, and your skin colour is beautiful.

I love your laughter. I laugh and look just like your mother.

I pray that you will continue to have good health and inspire the next generation.

You made sure that I attended school, because you were never given the chance.

I know that you are proud of me.

I am proud of you, too.

I love you, my queen Joy.

Loving Me

I love you.

I look in the mirror, taking notice of my reflection staring back at me,

Asking my mirror-self, "Do you love me?"

Waiting for her to answer me, as she waits also for me to answer her,

Thinking "What about me is there to love?"

When, from deep down, this still voice says,

"Everything." I ask with a shocked look on my face, "Everything?"

"Everything. I love you and I created you just like me, for me.

When you look in the mirror, I am the one that is looking back at you.

I have created you in my image, shaped and formed you in my love.

I have named every strand of hair on your head.

You are not a mistake; you were a good plan, and I am preparing you for my purpose.

I breathed life into you. I am the Bread of Life.

I am your loving Father. Your earthly father may not have shown you love,

But I am love, and I change not.

I know your weakness and your strength.

Keep in mind that when you are weak, I am strong.

Remember, I am with you always, not sometimes.

I am a promise maker and I am a promise keeper.

That's my name—Promise-keeping God

I will not fail you; I don't know how.

Believe in me, I am the God of truth,

I can't lie.

I wrote this poem about trusting in God and being honest with ourselves.

Second Time Around

I used to think that I knew what love was about
Until you came around.

You showed me what it meant to love and be loved.

You are my special love, the love I now believe in,

My gift from the Lord above, experiencing real love for the first time in my life.

I used to think that love was not for me, after all the betrayal and accusations that I have experienced.

My second time around in love, and it is so much better than the first time.

I'm just sorry that you weren't my first. We met at a time in my life when I had given up on love.

Thanks for coming into my life and not giving up on us. I love you.